Brilliant
and Crazy Inventions

Story by Claire Ubac

Factual accounts and
activities by Joël Lebeaume

contents

Story

Mega-infos

Activity

Mega-infos

Game

Mega-infos

Anecdotes

Mega-infos

Activity

Mega-infos

Quiz

Stickers

Picture Cards

Story

The Machine for Forgetting Time

The Twilight Blues

In the year 3098, in the tower that had become his symbol, the great industrialist Farou Arafon was finishing up his day. It was the moment he feared above all other times. He had his own name for it: The Twilight Blues.

All day long, he had studied files, consulted his partners, and run from meeting to meeting. And now the minutes

were wasting away uselessly. Boredom tortured Arafon. To escape it, he invented a new task for himself: devising a project that would keep him busier than all the other ones ever had before.

Just like that, back in 3095, he had come up with the idea to sell all animal feeds under the brand name Chanigou. In 3096, his women's underwear made out of nylotex was all the rage. In 3097, he got the monopoly on sales via the telerocket.

His agitation was worsening. From his desk, Arafon picked up the holograph of his father, who had died some years before. The man with a short mustache, standing before some unlikely plans for an interplanetary machine, was smiling at him. He had devoted his life to inventions. He came up with the craziest ideas, yet he never seemed to be working. He spent long hours contemplating the sand dunes outside. One day, Farou asked him the question that was burning in him: "What are you thinking about?"

His father answered softly, "You see, it's at these moments, when you seem like you're wasting your time, that you come up with the greatest ideas…"

Arafon shook his head to drive away that memory. Those words seemed as incomprehensible today as they did then. Moreover, with his eyes

fixed on the photo, his mind had already gone to work. He felt an idea coming that distracted him from his bad feeling: a means for commercializing ideas like those of his father.

"That's better than anything I've come up with yet," thought Arafon. "I'll get right on it!"

The next day, he announced his project to the media.

"Arafon Enterprises is creating a special factory. We'll build prototypes there by inventors from all over the galaxy! Each year, I myself will choose an invention to mass-produce."

The first year, Arafon chose an Enviro-nuclear bomb made from essence of flowers. It spread an intoxicating fragrance that would cause the aggressiveness of the enemy army to transform into brotherly love.

The following year, Arafon rewarded the work of a fourteen-year-old child crazy about interstellar kites. His ingenious system gathered clouds and caused nourishing rainfall on the driest areas of five planets.

The public, which had laughed at the prototypes, was soon convinced of their usefulness. The business project was under way.

Now Arafon would have to find something new to defeat his Twilight Blues…

The Secret of Isi ès

Arafon clapped his hands. The sliding door opened noiselessly. At the same time, Isi ès, her arm extended, received the signal to enter.

Arafon motioned for her to take a seat and asked her in a pleasant tone, "So, now you're making an appointment to see me?"

Isi ès expressed herself with an unexpected seriousness: "I have an invention to present to you. My own."

Arafon was caught by surprise. "A new one, then. You must have spent many nights on it!"

Isi ès handed him her file. She watched her boss intently, but he remained unaware. He murmured, absorbed in the pages, "The double-locomotus, a flexible means of transport. Let's see…Yes, it's ingenious."

Looking up, he startled the gray eyes staring at him. "It's good. I'll entrust you with taking care of developing the prototype yourself in the factory."

Story

Seeing the joy that swept across Isi ès's face, he felt that this was exactly what she had hoped for. How impassioned she seemed! Several times that day, the memory of his assistant's stare came to mind. What mystery was it hiding?

Several weeks later, he found this message from Isi ès on his work monitor: "Prototype ready. Meeting place: the planet Obo. Whenever you're ready." Arafon set aside a time for the very next day.

The Surprise

When Arafon arrived at the observation post, nary a cloud was obscuring the two suns of Obo; it was a glorious day. Farou Arafon thought about correcting an electronic file, then decided not to and leaned with his elbows on the railing. He let his gaze wander over the violet water. The color filled him with a peacefulness he had not felt in quite a long time.

He rubbed his eyes. An immense floating shape had just appeared at the edge of the horizon. It came majestically closer, revealing the details of its splendor. Arafon goggled his eyes. This mirage would collapse at a moment's notice and would

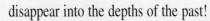

disappear into the depths of the past!

Someone lightly touched his arm. Arafon turned. Isi ès was watching him anxiously. Only then did he realize that it was her invention. For an instant, his mind was blank. Filled with the magical moment that he had just experienced, he was having trouble reassuming his role as the chief executive officer. Finally, he said in a flat tone, "What does this mean? This wasn't in the plans that you showed me!"

Contrary to all expectations, Isi ès burst out laughing. She cheerfully inquired, "What do you think of my surprise?"

The clever glint in her gray eyes dumbfounded her boss, while she began reciting verses by the great poet Yacine:

An immense palace glides o'er the waves
Its domes proffer their rotundity to the sun
Its windows cut into its towers
Open to the blue sky and the purple sea

An immense palace glides o'er the waves
As sublime and as bizarre
As an iceberg lost in the midst of the desert!

Arafon contemplated the floating palace, now quite near them. The contrast between its imposing bulk and the slight rock of the waves stirring it was fascinating. His assistant had succeeded in a technological feat comparable to having an elephant standing atop an eggshell!

He got ahold of himself and took Isi ès's arm with a firm gesture. "Let's take a closer look."

Together, they crossed the gangway to visit the prototype. Farou Arafon was speechless before the machinery filling the interior of the palace. It was made in an old style, with metals recycled from machines of the past. It was made up of thousands of wheelworks, some as large as the old motors of oil rigs, others, in contrast, as delicate as the mechanisms in automatons serving to measure time. It all ran ceaselessly, with a noise both delightful and archaic to ears of the thirty-first century.

The industrialist stared at the endless spirals drawn by the wheelworks, hypnotized. Isi ès, leaning against a pillar, watched him with an intense happiness. She had succeeded. He was as fascinated as a child! Finally, Arafon made an effort to remind himself of his responsibilities as an industrialist. He ran toward her.

"Tell me, what is your invention good for?"

She answered, after a moment of silence, "Why…nothing!"

Arafon repeated her, rolling the words around his mouth as though being able to savor them: "Nothing. Of course, nothing!"

His former discomfort was, in an instant, shattered by these simple words. He thought of his father. He would have liked to tell his father right then that his words of old now seemed so illuminating.

Leaning his head way back, Farou Arafon let out a liberating laugh.

Story by **Claire Ubac**
Illustrated by **Mouclier**

The Human Adventure

Tools do not grow on trees or in supermarkets. Who invented, imagined, and created them? Human beings, of course!

■ About Intelligence

Some birds sew, spiders weave, and other animals build. But only humans invent. Thanks to their intelligence, they search out, imagine, and create tools, instruments, and other things. From rocks, they made flints and, two million years later, they transformed sand into electronic components.

❦ *Clepsydra*
A water clock.

■ Always and Everywhere

Every great civilization made new things. The Egyptians invented perfume and the Greeks made maps. The Romans perfected faucets, the Arabs the **clepsydra**❦, and the Chinese brought into being gunpowder, paper, and the printing press.

■ Ingeniousness

In Europe, creative imagination burst forth during the Renaissance (sixteenth century). Engineers like Leonardo da Vinci devised war machines and lifting equipment in order to build monuments and palaces. They imagined diving gear, canal locks, bicycles, submarines, helicopters, parachutes... What geniuses!

■ The World Remains to Be Invented

The inventors of the past, if they could travel to our time, wouldn't recognize the world. The majority of inventions have been made over the last two centuries and inventions are more and more numerous. At this pace, what will the world be like tomorrow?

Incredible Ideas

That's new! Who ever saw such a thing!
It's extraordinary! Wow, what a great idea!
Someone had to think of it!

shears

■ Ideas from Earlier Ones...

❦ **Shears**
*Two blades joined
to form an opposing
action.*

Two cutting blades ending in rings and joined together form scissors. Much more practical than their predecessors, **shears**❦, they can be adapted to many uses. They become scissors for tailors, dressmakers, embroiderers...and even scissors for cutting boiled eggs.

■ Ideas That Are Finally Possible

Inventions are linked to scientific discoveries and technical possibilities. Thanks to electricity, for example, the vacuum cleaner has dethroned mechanical dusters: two bellows that housewives at the turn of the twentieth century would wear on their feet.

a duster

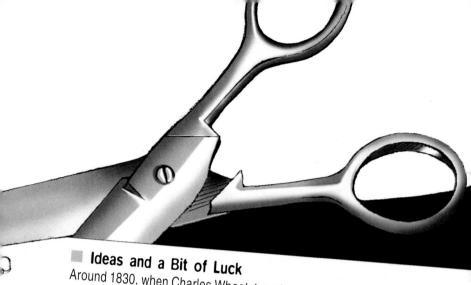

Ideas and a Bit of Luck

Around 1830, when Charles Wheatstone heard the echo of the vibrations of a violin in a stovepipe, he got the idea of a speaker. More recently, "Post-its" are the result of the invention of a poor-quality glue: When he needed some small page-markers for his songbook, Arthur Fry transformed the idea into a success.

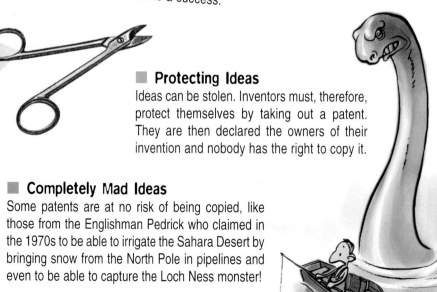

Protecting Ideas

Ideas can be stolen. Inventors must, therefore, protect themselves by taking out a patent. They are then declared the owners of their invention and nobody has the right to copy it.

Completely Mad Ideas

Some patents are at no risk of being copied, like those from the Englishman Pedrick who claimed in the 1970s to be able to irrigate the Sahara Desert by bringing snow from the North Pole in pipelines and even to be able to capture the Loch Ness monster!

The Shelf

Doctor Ayres' machine.

As Thomas Edison might have said, an invention is "one percent inspiration and ninety-nine percent perspiration." That is good to know.

■ Solutions Rediscovered

Around 100 CE, a Greek scientist, Hero of Alexandria, invented the first steam engine. With no practical use, it was merely a toy. In the nineteenth century, on the other hand, this machine became essential. Thomas Savery, Thomas Newcomen, and James Watt perfected it. This was the Industrial Revolution.

■ Temporary Failures

Certain inventions remained in the drawing stages. Doctor Ayres' machine was too heavy and could only remain on paper; his helices could turn no more than a few minutes. Too costly, other projects, such as the air train by the French engineer Jean Bertin, remained in the **prototype** stage. Maybe we will rediscover them one day.

❦ Prototype
First full-scale example of an invention.

for New Items

■ Perfecting

In 1893, the American Whitcomb Judson invented the slide fastener. But it took years of study to improve it and produce it industrially. The B. F. Goodrich Company called it the zipper. It was used to close the boots worn by American soldiers.

■ An Assembly Line of Inventions

One invention never comes about alone. The invention of the automobile also caused that of seat belts, roads, tires, street signs, drivers' licenses...and parking meters!

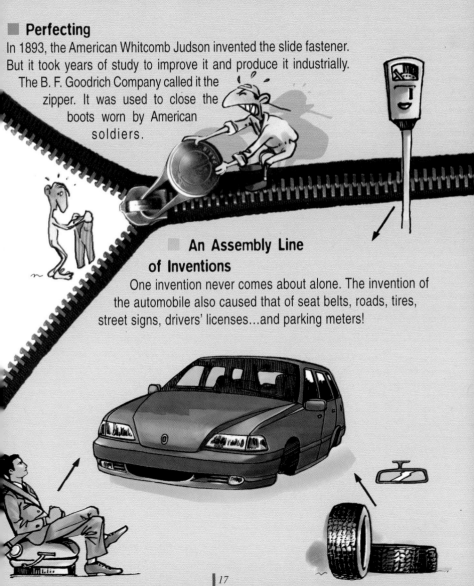

Making

Everyone knows what an egg is. But eggs in the form of a cube, that's a great invention!

1. Wash, rinse, and dry the cassette tape cases and the carton squares.

You will need:
- four cassette tape cases
- some adhesive tape
- a 2½-inch (6-cm) square and four 1½-inch (4-cm) squares, cut from a milk carton
- a lid from a bottle of water
- some eggs
- a full can of canned goods
- a pot

3. With an adult's help, put two eggs into a pot of boiling water. Take them out after nine minutes; they'll be hard. Remove the shells while they're still hot.

2. With the adhesive tape, assemble the cassette tape cases to make a mold of 1½ inches (4 cm) on each side. Glue the large carton square on the bottom.

4. Place an egg in the mold, then two small squares, and finally the second egg.

Activity
Cubed Eggs

5. Cover the mold with the two remaining squares and press down, using the lid to help you.

6. Put everything in the refrigerator and put the can on top. Take the eggs out of the mold when they're cold. What animal could have laid them?

It's a why,

It is not found in nature and yet it seems so natural to us. Mounted on an axle, the wheel is one of the inventions it would be impossible to do without.

■ Carrying, Pulling, Rolling

For a long time, loads were carried on animals' backs, on sleds, and on rollers. Then someone came up with a really great idea: Create a vehicle equipped with a platform, an **axle**☜, and one or more wheels. This invention goes back, no doubt, to 3000 years BCE, well after the invention of weaving, boats, or the plow.

☜ *Axle*
A bar that links two wheels.

The sail wagon of Simon Stévin (17th century).

■ Wagons

Wagons pushed or pulled by men or animals then replaced sleds. But which solution was to be adopted: two wheels fixed on an axle that turns or, rather, two free wheels on a fixed axle? The second one, because it is the only one that allows for curves!

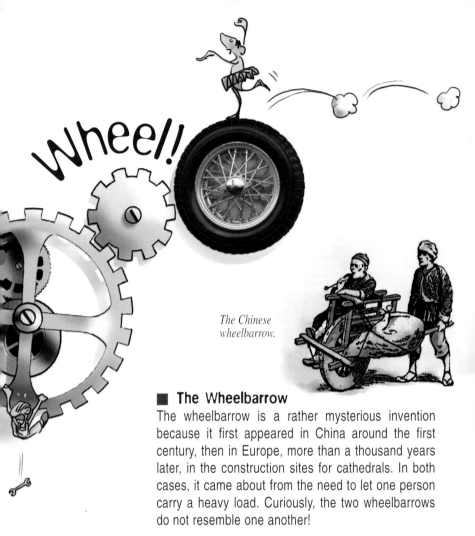

Wheel!!

The Chinese wheelbarrow.

■ The Wheelbarrow

The wheelbarrow is a rather mysterious invention because it first appeared in China around the first century, then in Europe, more than a thousand years later, in the construction sites for cathedrals. In both cases, it came about from the need to let one person carry a heavy load. Curiously, the two wheelbarrows do not resemble one another!

■ The Elastic Wheel

On paved or unpaved highways, what a jolting! Around 1850, someone finally had the idea of gluing a layer of rubber onto wheels, then of tires inflated with air. But flats were frequent and people were scared of tires. The invention of the wheel with elastic bands raised brief hopes, but it was not a success. They snapped!

Mega-infos

They Go All

Equipped with three or four wheels, every vehicle becomes more stable. And if a way could be found for the vehicle to go all by itself, it would be an "auto"-mobile!

Farffler's automobile (1685).

■ First Attempts

Instead of being pulled by an animal, an automobile must carry the energy that allows it to go. At the end of the Middle Ages, a first model was powered by the action of arms. It could not, alas, go any faster than a pedestrian. Someone also thought of putting sails on carts. These were the predecessors of pedal cars and sail wagons.

Cugnot's road wagon.

■ The Gas Engine

Steam-driven vehicles on the ground did not succeed very well either. Joseph Cugnot's "road wagon" (1770) was so heavy, this thing resembling a pot of boiling water atop three wheels could not go forward. It was necessary to await the invention of the gasoline engine in 1885 for cars really to work. But people did not realize that, at the same time, they were inventing…traffic jams!

By Themselves

A car equipped with elastic tires.

🖤 **Combustible**
Something that has the ability to produce energy when burning.

■ A Century of Progress

Progress cannot be stopped! Engineers have perfected natural-gas motors, a **combustible**🖤 that pollutes less than does gasoline. Electric cars are already available. As for a solar car, we will have to wait for some more technical advances: lighter materials, powerful solar cells...And how do you make one work at night?

23

At Last,

A frame and two wheels is a bicycle, obviously! For a very long time, however, no one had yet thought of it and, in its early days, it was only an amusing curiosity.

■ Two Wheels

Put two wheels one behind the other, that was the revolutionary idea that gave birth in 1790 to the "celeripede." Thanks to the movable front wheel, it could turn. In France, it was named the "Draisienne" celeripede after its inventor, Karl Friedrich Drais. Truly a promising solution, much better than Sievier's pedal machine with its two parallel wheels!

■ Two Pedals

With pedals, you can go a lot faster. In 1839, MacMillan's **velocipede🐾** was the first to be equipped with them, but it was a very complicated mechanism. Some twenty years later, Macmillan thought of connecting them directly to the front wheel. What an advantage, especially on slopes! To go even faster, it was only necessary to enlarge the diameter of the wheel. The tall "Ordinary" was invented in 1870.

> 🐾 *Velocipede* means a man with fast feet.

Sievier's pedal machine, around 1810.

the Bicycle!

■ A Chain

With a chain, the pedals draw along the rear tire on the modern bicycle. Numerous accessories quickly bettered its performance. Over time, certain inventors added to it propellers and a motor. It then becomes a "velomotor," a moped, or even a rocket-bike—a motor that goes as fast as 124 miles (200 km) per hour. Others study the solution for laying back—it's more comfortable and less dangerous in case of a fall.

■ A "Climbing" Cycle

Invented by a German in 1929, this bicycle does not climb hills, but rather goes up poles and tree trunks! It is one example of the many adaptations of the bicycle.

The Ordinary.

Essential Inventions

1

the plow
3500 BCE

the wheel
3000 BCE

the light bulb
1879

the telephone
1876

7

the automobile
1885

8

the vacuum cleaner 1901

the airpla
1903

All of these inventions have been ranked from the most ancient to the most recent, except for ten, at the bottom of the page, that the illustrator did not know how to classify. Can you put them where they belong?

Answers on page 63.

A
the toothbrush

B
glasses

C
television

D
the subma

Game

clepsydra
300 BCE

scissors
500 BCE

3

gunpowder
1250

4

the microscope
1590

5

elocipede
1839

the battery
1800

the parachute
1797

the steamship
1783

6

the telescope
1663

9

ballpoint pens
1943

the computer
1945

10

compact discs
1979

E
ving

F
the robot

G
jeans

H
skis

I
the compass

J
the zipper

27

Walks on

Crossing rivers without getting wet, what imagination! If only we could walk on water!

Clara-Louisa Wells' water skis.

■ Water Skis

With your feet covered in long floats, you can walk on water. Well, almost...In 1915, Clara-Louisa Wells took out a patent to improve these water skis: a motor, a hat filled with air, a jacket with rows of small buoys, and sticks to keep your balance. The equipment is also available for dogs!

■ An Amphibious ❧ Cycle

What if the wheels floated? That was the idea of the Englishman Pinkert, who, in 1894, invented the water velocipede. Thanks to the little blades on its wheels, it moves along rapidly. There is nothing more practical for going from dry land into the water.

> ❧ *Amphibious*
> *Can be used on the ground and in the water.*

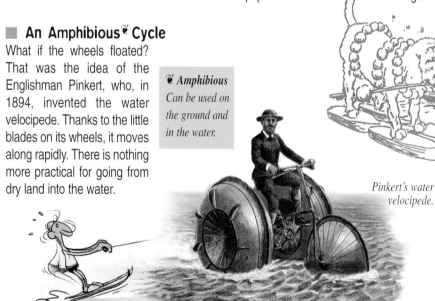

Pinkert's water velocipede.

---

the Water

The aquatic tripod.

■ The Aquatic Tripod

With its three floats attached to the saddle, it looks like a water spider. This is the aquatic tripod, invented by...someone unknown. Particularly quiet, it is recommended for hunters, on the condition, of course, that they walk without making any noise!

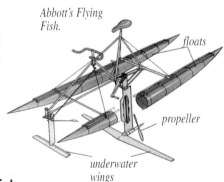

Abbott's Flying Fish.

floats

propeller

underwater wings

■ The Flying Fish

Allan Abbott, an American inventor, baptized it the "flying fish," but it is really a kind of bicycle-boat. Thanks to its propeller and its underwater wings, called "hydrofoils," it takes off at 6 miles (10 km) an hour and can approach speeds of 25 miles (40 km) an hour. When will it break the speed record?

Underwater:

The record for free diving🐟 while holding your breath is around eight minutes. To remain underwater longer, take along a supply of breathable air!

> 🐟 *Free diving*
> *Diving without breathing gear.*

A Real Problem

Excessive depth can prove fatal to divers. At more than 35 feet (10 m), the pressure of the water is such that one can only breathe compressed air. It is impossible, therefore, to use breathing tubes connected to the open air or to use diving bells.

A diving bell (1676).

Hard-hat Rigs

Called "hard-hat rigs," these heavy diving suits were equipped with shoes made from lead, a "bucket" helmet with a front window, and a pipe connected to a tube producing compressed air. Around 1850, with the invention of the Rouquayrol-Denayrousse portable apparatus, this quite cumbersome tube went out of use. Henceforth, divers carried along their supply of air.

This survival suit can contain a two-month supply of food and water and protects against hungry fish!

It's Not Easy!

■ The Frogman

Although cylinders of compressed air had been invented, they were difficult to use until the **regulator*** was perfected by the engineer Gagnan and the future commander Jacques Cousteau. Finally, after 1947, the air began to be regulated automatically based on the diver's breathing rate and on the depth of the dive. The frogman was born!

🛎 *Regulator*
A device that changes air pressure automatically.

■ On Board Submarines

With air tanks, it is not possible to dive deeper than 170 feet (50 m) below the surface. The bottom of the ocean is more than 6 miles (10 km) deep. Only a few submarines can reach these extreme depths. What marvelous inventions they are, beginning with the astonishing undertaking of the American David Bushnell in 1776, in his all-too-slow Turtle with its hand-driven propellers, down to the future generation of the Deep Flight, piloted by a man lying flat on his stomach. He can see the ground.

Bushnell's Turtle.

Deep Flight.

Free as a Bird

Lana's Flying Boat (1670).

Flying is an ageless dream that has inspired many marvelous flying madmen, but...it was a nightmare for some who only succeeded in crashing to the ground!

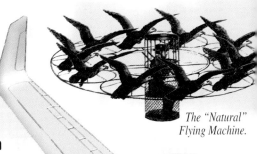

The "Natural" Flying Machine.

■ Much Imagination

With feathers glued to their arms or by commanding a machine equipped with beating wings, people could become birds. Alas, the idea was a false one and a guaranteed failure. Imagine oneself being carried along by eagles in this flying machine designed in 1865!

The aerostat, functioning via manual force (1843).

Mega-infos

The First Flying Machines

When people began to understand the principles of
aerodynamics ❦, two solutions appeared: from around
1780, devices that were lighter than air—from vessels
supported by soap bubbles to the Montgolfier brothers' hot-air
balloon; and, a century later, devices that were heavier than
air—gliders and planes. But, oh, the number of broken wings and
crash landings before the success of flight!

> ❦ *Aerodynamics*
> *The study of the*
> *movement of an*
> *object in the air.*

The Solutions of Nature

Even though it is impossible to fly like a bird, the
observation of nature contributed to much progress.
Thus, the seed of the maple tree is at the origin of the
invention of aerial propellers, and the bat inspired the
wings of Otto Lilienthal's glider and those of
Clément Ader's Aeolus, the first airplane.

*Clément Ader's
airplane, the
Aeolus.*

Airplanes of Tomorrow

Future airplanes will perhaps be rocket planes flying
through space at more than 15,500 miles (25,000 km)
per hour, giant wings carrying more than a thousand
passengers, or...ultralight pedaling machines!

Your Head in the Stars

The sky, the planets, and the stars, so many worlds to conquer! But how do you get there, then return without getting lost in infinite space?

Flaming Arrows

After having invented gunpowder, the Chinese became experts in the art of **pyrotechnics ❦**. Well before the first millenium, they were launching fireworks and flaming arrows into the sky. The fireworks were the first rockets and the ancestors of missiles.

> ❦ *Pyrotechnics*
> *The art of making and using fireworks.*

Astronauts

According to Chinese legend, around 1500, Wan-Hu was the first astronaut. But the unfortunate man did not survive the explosion of the battery of rockets to which he was attached! Others have had more luck since then. In 1961, the Russian cosmonaut Yuri Gagarin made the first complete spatial orbit around the Earth. He returned safely in his capsule.

And If We Could Live There?

Going out into space is a feat made possible by the invention of the space suit, a veritable shell that protects against cosmic rays, extremely variable (mostly cold) temperatures, and blows from meteorites and provides air to breathe. Being able to live for several months in orbital stations is another step in progress: great vacations for the future!

The Sojourner robot.

Dreams of the Unknown

Making it to the moon fed the imagination. In 1969, the rocket *Apollo XI* carried Neil Armstrong and Buzz Aldrin there. They walked on the moon 104 years after Jules Verne's explorers in *From the Earth to the Moon*. Recently, the Sojourner robot trod the soil of Mars. Will it discover traces of the little green men from **science fiction** novels?

> ℰ **Science fiction**
> *A genre of novels or movies that imagines things that are scientifically possible.*

35

Incredible

● Animals First!

In order to test certain inventions, people have preferred animals. The first flight of the Montgolfier brothers' balloon, a few years before the French Revolution (1789), was carried out by a sheep, a rooster, and a duck. The *Sputnik* flight in 1957 made the little dog Laïka famous.

■ *Hats Off?*

Many inventors are unknown, but some have left their name with their invention. Eugène Poubelle, the head of the Seine department, made the use of metallic boxes obligatory for French people, who call their trash cans "poubelles." Lord Sandwich, always in a hurry, too to his office a meal that has since kept his nam John Loudon MacAdam bettered the condition of roadways with a coat of gravel and crushed stones covered in tar: macadam.

but True!

■ What a Jokester!

When Thomas Edison introduced his
invention the phonograph, the first device
for recording and playing back the human
voice, the public did not take him seriously,
thinking he was a ventriloquist.

● Mysteries!

Leonardo da Vinci drew and annotated his
inventions in little notebooks, called the
Codex. Curiously, they are written in
reverse: Leonardo was left-handed
and wrote from right to left, perhaps
in order to not reveal his ideas. It is
also said that he inspired the majority
of inventions in subsequent centuries.
How could this be possible, since his
Codex books were only rediscovered at the
end of the nineteenth century?

Fascinating Automatons

These automatons with their painstakingly practiced gestures and with their constantly repeated motions are true marvels. They are the grandparents of robots!

■ Spectacles for the Sake of Pleasure

Theater lovers, the Greeks created stage-sets where the characters elegantly came alive on their own, thanks to perfected mechanisms. Even more astonishingly, Hero of Alexandria designed a temple with automatic doors: A fire made them open, and, when the fire went out, the doors closed.

■ Waterworks

What a spectacle fountains and water jets were in princely gardens! And what genius was necessary to invent the pumps that powered them. The most incredible was the machine by Marly ordered by Louis XIV for his palace in Versailles. The cost was extreme and the machine barely worked.

■ Curiosities

Regulated by clock mechanisms, automatons attempt to reproduce the mechanics of living beings. In the eighteenth century, Jacques de Vaucanson's duck digested the grain that it ate. In the nineteenth century, Phalibois's conjuring machine made his head disappear, then reappear. Like magic!

■ A Change of Program!

The first automatons could only perform their motions in a closed cycle. With the invention of Vaucanson's perforated cards, their program could be changed. Barrel organs also played different melodies "at will" and the cloth works could then make any kind of fabric pattern: You only had to change the card.

Vaucanson's duck.

Extreme

The first computer was born in 1948. Since then, information is everything. It is the revolution of the third millennium.

■ Robots

Robots truly resemble us. They play on an organ reading from sheet music, serve in restaurants, and carry medicine in hospitals. They even take the elevator.

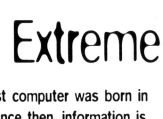

Intelligence

■ Something New Every Day

Invented in 1902, an alarm that rings, then lights an alcohol lamp, boils water, prepares tea, and signals when everything is ready foreshadows the automatic house. The house is completely controlled by a computer: The shutters close themselves at night, the televisions turn on and off with the movements of the family, the watering of the plants is done.... This has been around since 1980.

■ Factories without People

All the tedious, dangerous, and repetitive tasks in factories are performed by industrial robots. In car plants, they paint, weld, and install dashboards. They move about, cross paths, and stop under the commands of powerful computers controlling this ballet. What workers they are!

■ The Robotic Freeway

Magnets and cameras on the freeway, sensors in all vehicles, and all information transmitted via satellite to a central computer: That is the highway of the future currently being tested in California. No more traffic jams and accidents, and no more need for a steering wheel. The cars run all by themselves...in single file.

A robot for welding car shocks.

Knowing Infinity

Talking, expressing oneself, learning, sharing ideas and feelings, all that is communication.

Dom Gauthey's telephone (1782).

■ Limitless Knowledge

The Chinese invented **movable type❦**. Thanks to Johannes Gutenberg's invention of the printing press, knowledge is reproduced, multiplied, and made available. Everything is transmitted and can be learned. In the twentieth century, with radio, television, and fax machines, you can no longer remain ignorant. Everything may be known immediately.

> ❦ *Movable type*
> *Metal letters used in printing.*

Distance No Longer Matters

In 1782, Dom Gauthey successfully communicated with a person almost a mile (km) away at the other end of a pipe. This lead pipe telephone, of course, did not have any future! However, scarcely a hundred years later, the telegraph and then the electric telephone invented by Alexander Graham Bell began the era of telecommunications.

Mega-infos

■ Web Surfers

http@communication.ed: A code is the only thing needed to open the doors to the world of information. At the close of the twentieth century, web surfers consult their mailboxes and e-mail. On the Internet, they can shop in a **virtual** store to make a few purchases, browse in the worldwide library to find a document, and even review in school for their tests!

☙ **Virtual**
It does not exist.

■ Virtual Reality

The DataGlove, invented in 1982, is a glove connected to a computer. There is no longer any need for an instrument to play the guitar; gestures of the hand suffice! And with head-mounted displays, you are actually plunged into an unreal world where synthesized images follow your slightest movements. A virtual world from an armchair!

Mega-infos

Even Smaller

Even while they are "growing up," inventions are becoming increasingly smaller and tinier...even disappearing!

■ A Mammoth

The mammoth was a camera weighing more than 1,500 pounds (700 kg) built around 1900 to get a detailed photograph of a train. At the end of the 1990's, everything is so tiny, a camera can be installed on the back of a remote-controlled insect. This roach-spy is essential in espionage and in searching for victims of earthquakes.

The mammoth.

❦ Miniaturization
The process of making something as small as possible.

Chips

In the second half of the twentieth century, the transistor, the integrated circuit, and the microprocessor are the most important inventions ensuring the **miniaturization❦** of devices. They launched the invasion of cards with memory chips, phone cards, bank cards, and medical cards. A giant leap forward!

The roach-spy.

44

Mega, Mini, Micro

The ENIAC, the first computer, performed 300 operations a second, but it weighed more than 30 tons and took up approximately the space of a basketball court. Since 1945, the computer has become miniaturized, then micro-sized, while considerably increasing in speed and memory capacity. What a huge invention!

Hyper, Super, Extra

A hand-held television, headphones, a telephone in one hand, a computer in the other, the head-mounted display acting as virtual glasses...the complete outfit for the person of the year 2000 comes in all sizes!

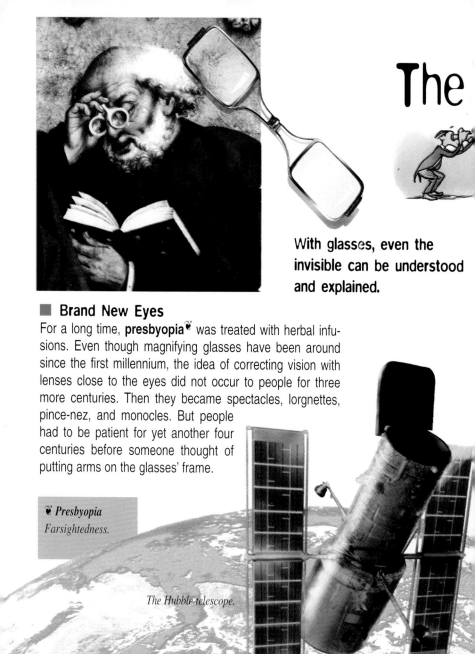

The

With glasses, even the invisible can be understood and explained.

Brand New Eyes

For a long time, **presbyopia*** was treated with herbal infusions. Even though magnifying glasses have been around since the first millennium, the idea of correcting vision with lenses close to the eyes did not occur to people for three more centuries. Then they became spectacles, lorgnettes, pince-nez, and monocles. But people had to be patient for yet another four centuries before someone thought of putting arms on the glasses' frame.

*** Presbyopia**
Farsightedness.

The Hubble telescope.

Transparent World

Wig spectacles (18th century).

Seeing Well in All Conditions

Seeing at night is easy with infrared glasses. If the light is too strong, it is better to wear sunglasses. And why not offer the same comfort to our favorite animals? That is what Denise Lemière proposed in 1975.

A microscope from the 17th century.

Infinitely Small

The world changed with the invention of the microscope. Cells were discovered in 1610. The function of spermatozoid and the birth of children could then be explained. Better-perfected, the electron microscope allowed the discovery of an ever smaller world, such as that of mites, the microscopic creatures that live with us.

Infinitely Great

Galileo, by creating a star-glass in 1609, found proof that Earth turns. Nowadays, giant telescopes like the Hubble, carried on satellites more than 370 miles (600 km) from Earth, are discovering new galaxies. We are beginning to see the universe differently.

Mites as seen with a microscope.

Strange

Thanks to glasses with two slits invented by the Eskimos, the sun is blinding, nor is the light bouncing of the snow.

You will need:
- cardboard
- a ruler
- a pencil
- a pair of scissors
- a utility knife
- paint or old magazines

Sunglasses

1. Trace the glasses in the desired shape. Do not forget the space between the eyes and the frame-arms. Then cut out the shape.

2. Trace the slits. Ask an adult to cut them out with the knife.

3. Decorate it as you like with paint or with magazine photos. You come up with the style!

Everyday Things

We are so accustomed to them, we do not even think about them! But if they did not exist, they would need to be invented.

Chewing gum 1869
W. S. Simple
(United States)

hamburger 1850s
german immigrants
(United States)

blue jeans 1850
O. Levi-Strauss
(United States)

Walkman 1979
Akio Morita
(japan)

lego® 1958
g. K. Christiansen
(Denmark)

Mega-infos

hand soap 1791
n. leblanc
(france)

teddy bear 1902
marguerite sreiff
(germany)

pencils 1792
nicolas conté
(france)

kleenex 1924
Kimberly-Clark Co.
(United States)

barbie doll 1958
Mattel Co.
(United States)

Silly, Unheard-of...

With imagination, common sense, and lots of audacity, Jacques Carelman invents unheard-of things. What an artist!

■ Suppertime!

Forks, with just two prongs, first appeared on tables only in the sixteenth century. Carelman's spaghetti forks will make for a complete set!

Spaghetti fork.

■ Watch Out, It's Hot!

The coffeepot was invented at the same time as the coffee grinder in the sixteenth century. With Carelman's **masochist's** ❤ coffeepot, it's impossible not to burn yourself!

A masochist's coffee pot.

> ❤ **Masochist**
> Someone who likes to suffer.

■ It Will Pull Your Hair Out!

Combs date back into pre-history. A bald-man's comb by Carelman is a lot more recent!

A bald-man's comb.

Mega-infos

■ On the Tips of Your Toes

Joseph Merlin invented roller skates in 1759. Two centuries later, for people crazy about speed, they are equipped with a motor. Carelman, for his part, is thinking about ballerinas: To stand on their toes, one wheel is enough!

Roller skates for classical dance.

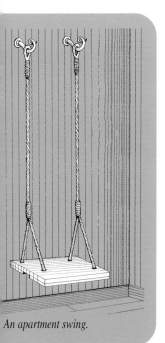

An apartment swing.

■ One-Way Trips!

The swing is a very ancient means of amusement. Carelman proposes a model for small apartments, to be attached to a wall.

The economic "Elephant" faucet.

■ Drop by Drop

When the Englishman Thomas Grill invented the modern faucet in 1800, he also invented drips. With an economic model he calls the "Elephant," Carelman has definitively solved that problem!

That Might Hurt!

Certain ideas can hurt, but for someone's own good. Others only hurt. Watch out for excessively absurd deviations!

■ Owww, Ouch, That Stings!

The syringe might well sting, but it also cures. Invented around 1850, it is one of the instruments of modern medicine. At last, we have remedies that are less dangerous than being sick!

■ Crack!

The fingers of pianists must be capable of particularly supple movements. How can they be loosened and exercised? Use, for instance, this Swedish machine, invented to stretch and strengthen the fingers.

The Swedish machine.

Mega-infos

A corset from around 1830.

■ It Takes Away Your Breath

Having the waistline of a wasp was in style in the nineteenth century. The corset creates this shape that is so pleasing to the eye, but at the cost of a real deformation of the body. It was difficult to breathe, especially when it was tightened with a hand crank.

■ What Violence!

Louis XI is well known for the punishments inflicted on prisoners in his dungeons, holes in which they could not even stand upright. And with pointed collars and manacles, it was impossible to move.

Black Humor

The black glasses imagined by Spoerri, with needles glued into the interior of the lenses, make you laugh more than cry. Just like the cork remover resembling a cactus that Jean-Paul Balou proposes.

Curious

The majority of machines are useful. But sometimes invention comes up with almost useless contraptions!

To Tell the Truth

The invention of the lie detector, in 1921, relied on scientific studies that show that the heartbeat and breathing change when someone lies. All the same, this machine needs a great deal of perfecting in order to be reliable!

As Stupid as Ever!

Since learning is not always very easy, why not help students by creating machines that could program their movements or would stuff them with the sum of knowledge? The answers have not yet been discovered. Fortunately!

On paper, the billiards should drive the wh... and the mechanism sufficiently to make them go back up. It is impossible because of friction

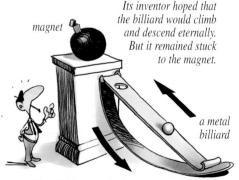

Its inventor hoped that the billiard would climb and descend eternally. But it remained stuck to the magnet.

magnet

a metal billiard

Really Impossible

Inventors have deployed the treasures of imagination in order to create a perpetual motion that could ensure the eternal functioning of machines. Alas, it is impossible to make something work out of nothing.

Discoveries

■ Watch Out for Spankings!

In the glorious era of the steam engine, someone even imagined a machine…for spankings. It is powered with toys taken away from children!

Gaston Lagaffe's machine for making paper airplanes.

■ Crazy Machines

Many machines remain to be invented and built: to fabricate paper airplanes, to cut hair into four parts, to pull ears, to dream…. There is no lack of ideas. Gaston Lagaffe and many others are thinking about them!

Quiz

True or

■ **At the end of his reign, Louis XIV could have worn glasses.**

True. Glasses (with frame-arms) appeared around 1700.

■ **Louis Rustine invented the Rustine rubber patch**

Pshht!

True.

■ **Telling someone that he's not a real whiz is a compliment.**

False. It means they're not very intelligent.

■ **Inventors sometimes get their ideas from observing nature.**

True. For example, the maple seed inspired the propeller.

58

False?

■ **Jules Verne based his book *From the Earth to the Moon* on the first trip to the moon.**

False. That adventure preceded Neil Armstrong's steps on the moon (1969) by more than one hundred years.

■ **A clock that's stopped can still tell time.**

■ **As soon as the wheel was invented, the bicycle was born.**

False. More than four thousand years separate the invention of the wheel from that of the bicycle.

True. It indicates the correct time only two times a day!

Phew

■ **In space, astronauts use suits so they don't get cold.**

True. The suits provide temperature control as well as breathable air.

Ah, well! *Quiz*

True or

■ By taking out a patent, the inventor becomes the owner of his or her invention.

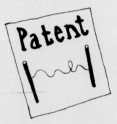

True. It is the means for proving that he or she was the first one to have the idea.

■ In the beginning, "velocipede" meant "a six-pedal machine."

False. "Velocipede" means (man) "with rapid feet."

■ Hero of Alexandria's steam engine was used in cooking.

False. His machine wasn't used for anything.

■ The lie detector is a machine that always reveals the truth.

TRUE

False. It, too, can lie! The heartbeat does not change only when one is lying.

False?

■ **Automatons were invented to make the work of humans less tedious.**

False. In the beginning, they had no other function than amusing spectators...and proving the power of the king.

■ **Thanks to the regulator invented by Jacques Cousteau, people can reach the bottom of the seas.**

False. It permitted people to move more freely while diving, but a submarine is required to go deeper than 170 feet (50 m).

■ **The first cars were frightening.**

GRRR

True. To warn people, a man on foot would go ahead of them on the road with a flag...himself going 3 miles (5 km) per hour.

■ **In 1998, pow-dered water was finally invented.**

H_2O

False. This invention hasn't yet come about and never will!

Index

Answers to the game on pages 26–27

Answers: A6 ; B4 ; C9 ; D5 ; E1 ; F10 ; G7 ; H2 ; I3 ; J8.

1780   ca. 1280   1929   1620   7000 BCE   1962   1850   2500 BCE   ca. 1200   1891

Photo credits

Activities: F. Hanoteau / Nathan.

Stickers: Archives Nathan; Cat's collection; Cat's collection; Archives Nathan / Coll. J.-Michel Arnold; Col. Kharbine-Tapabor; Archives Nathan; Bibliothèque Nationale; J. Carelman; Mary Evans / Archives Explorer; Archives Nathan; Mary Evans / Archives Explorer; Gamma / Sander-Liaison.

Picture cards (left to right): **Top:** Renault Communication; Cosmos / SPL-Scharf; Archives Nathan; Bibliothèque Nationale; Archives Nathan; Archives Nathan. **Bottom:** Bibliothèque Nationale; Cosmos / SPL-Nasa; Léonard © Dargaud Éditeur, par Turk & De Groot; Archives Nathan / Col. J.-Michel Arnold; Eurolios / Plailly; Cat's Collection.

P. 28: Bibliothèque Nationale; p. 50: Lego®: reprinted with the permission of Lego France, © 1998 Groupe Lego; p. 51: Barbie: © Mattel Inc.; pp. 52-53: Jacques Carelman; p. 57: Gaston Lagaffe © Éditions Dupuis, 1973.

Illustrations

Daniel Guerrier, Martin Matje, Olivier Nadel. **Cover:** Olivier Nadel.

©1998 by Editions Nathan, Paris, France
The title of the French edition is *Inventions géniales et délirantes*.
Published by Les Editions Nathan, Paris.
English translation © Copyright 1999 by Barron's Educational Series, Inc.

All inquiries should be addressed to:

Barron's Educational Series, Inc.
250 Wireless Boulevard
Hauppauge, New York, 11788
http://www.barronseduc.com

Library of Congress Catalog Card No.: 98-74450
International Standard Book No.: 0-7641-5183-5

Printed in Italy
9 8 7 6 5 4 3 2 1

Stickers

R2-D2 and C-3PO
in Star Wars

Drais' celeripede

A Chinese
wheelbarrow
with sails

A Whale-bus

A plan for a balloon (1784)   *Sievier's machine*

Stickers

The cat handbag
by Jacques Carelman

A car that
vacuums up
careless pedestrians

The "decacycle," a bicycle built for ten

An environmental
helmet

Edison's

Titles in the Megascope series:

The Adventures of the Great Explorers

Amazing Nature

Brilliant and Crazy Inventions

Infinite Space

Life in the Middle Ages

Mysteries, True and False

Our Planet Earth

The Pharaohs of Ancient Egypt

Searching for Human Origins

Understanding the Human Body

BARRON'S